PLAN

Peter

034

W
FRANKLIN WATTS
LONDON • SYDNEY

This edition 2003

Franklin Watts
96 Leonard Street
London EC2A 4XD

Franklin Watts Australia
45–51 Huntley Street
Alexandria
NSW 2015

© Franklin Watts 1998
Text © Peter Riley 1998

Series editor: Sarah Snashall
Designer: Mo Choy
Art director: Robert Walster
Picture research: Sue Mennell and
Alex Young
Photography: Steve Shott (unless
otherwise credited)
Artwork: Peter Bull

A CIP catalogue record for this book
is available from the British Library.
Dewey Decimal Classification 581.1

ISBN 0 7496 5219 5

Printed in Belgium

Picture credits:
Bruce Coleman pp. 5b (H. Reinhard),
10t (Dr. E. Pott), 16b (E. Crichton),
29t (T. Buchholz); Garden Picture
Library pp. 4l (J. Glover), 12t
(R. Sutherland); Frank Lane Picture
Agency pp. 5m (H. Clark), 6
(W. Broadhurst), 9t (M. Nimmo), 14b
(Life Science Images), 18b
(R.P. Lawrence), 26t (G.E. Hyde);
Holt Studios International pp. cover
(N. Cattlin), 14t (N. Cattlin), 23r
(N. Cattlin), 24b (N. Cattlin), 29b (N.
Cattlin); Natural History Photographic
Agency pp. 5t (G.J. Cambridge), 8t
(M.I. Walker), 19r (S. Dalton); Oxford
Scientific Films pp. 8b (H. Taylor), 9b
(H. Taylor), 11t (C. Milkins), 13bl
(G.I. Bernard), 15t (London Scientific
Films), 18t (Animals Animals/Breck
P. Kent), 19l (M. Leach), 20m
(D. Wright), 22t (H. Taylor), 22b
(G.I. Bernard), 23l (London Scientific
Films), 26b (H. Taylor), 27t (G.A.
Maclean), 27m (G.I. Bernard), 27b
(R. Day); Derek Whitford p. 13tl.

CONTENTS

A WORLD OF PLANTS

There are thousands of different kinds of plant. They can be found in most places on the Earth. Some tiny plants float in the sunlit waters of seas and lakes. Others live on the sea shore but most live on land.

WHAT IS A PLANT?

A plant is a living thing that uses the energy in sunlight to make its own food. Plants have many different features. Some plants have a root to secure them to a certain place in the ground. Some have a shoot made up of a stem, leaves and sometimes flowers. Some plants reproduce by making seeds, other plants make spores. Spores and seeds grow into new plants. We use these features to put plants into groups.

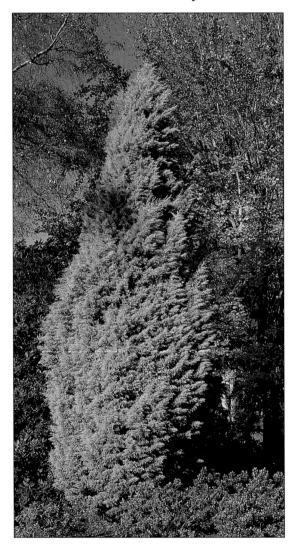

Conifer leaves are thin and waxy and grow all year round.

FLOWERING PLANTS

Flowering plants are the most common type of plant. They have roots, stems, leaves and flowers. The flowers make seeds.

Many flowering plants can be grown in pots.

CONIFERS

Conifers are trees. They have roots and a shoot with a stem and leaves. Most conifers breed by making seeds in cones. The largest living thing on Earth is a conifer tree called a Giant Sequoia.

FERNS

Ferns have roots, stems and large leaves called fronds. On the underside of the frond are dark lumps which release spores into the air.

Many ferns grow in shady places in woods.

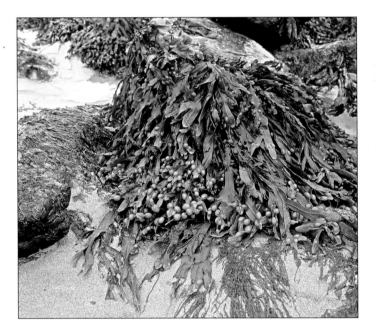

ALGAE

Algae do not have stems, leaves or proper roots. They live in water or on damp surfaces of rocks and breed by producing spores. Most algae are so small that they can only be seen with a microscope. Some live together in colonies which can be seen as a green patch.

The largest types of algae are the sea weeds.

MOSSES

Mosses have stems and leaves but they do not have proper roots. They grow on rocks, tree stumps and on the surface of the soil. When moss plants breed, a stalk with a swollen tip called a capsule grows above the leaves. The capsule releases spores which are carried away by the air currents.

Moss plants are only a few centimetres high.

FLOWERING PLANTS

The body of a flowering plant is divided into two parts. They are the root and the shoot. The root grows in the ground and the shoot grows above it in the air or along the ground.

ROOTS

The roots hold the plant in the ground. They stop it from being blown away by a strong wind or from being pulled out of the soil by an animal.

The root takes up water from the soil. Each root has tiny hairs along part of its length. They grow out between the soil particles and collect water covering their surfaces. When the roots take up water, they also take up minerals that are dissolved in the water. The minerals are chemicals that help the plant to grow.

This tree is held in the bank by its strong roots.

THE SHOOT

The shoot is made up of a stem, leaves, buds and flowers. There is a large bud at the tip of the shoot and smaller buds down its sides. The shoot increases its length when the bud at the tip bursts open. A stem with leaves and one or more flowers grows out of the bud.

When the side buds burst open, they form side shoots with leaves and flowers. A side bud grows just above the place where a leaf sprouts from the stem.

This branch of an apple tree grew from a bud. Further side shoots are growing out of the branch.

INVESTIGATE!

Look at a shoot and find the buds next to the leaves.
Examine the way buds and leaves are arranged along the shoot.

A CLOSER LOOK AT PLANTS

If you look at a piece of a plant under the microscope, you will see that it is made of tiny 'boxes'. Each 'box' is called a cell. There are different kinds of cell in a plant. Each kind of cell has a special task in keeping the plant alive.

A nucleus can be seen in most of the cells of this magnified piece of onion skin.

THE CONTROL CENTRE OF A CELL

In a cell, there is a spot of material called a nucleus. The nucleus controls the activities of the cell and keeps it alive.

CELLS THAT SUPPORT THE STEM

The centre of the stem is filled with large cells. The cells hold water and this makes the stem firm so that the leaves can spread out to catch light from the sun. If the cells do not have enough water, the stem collapses and we say that the plant has wilted.

The cells in the middle of this stem are much larger than the cells around the edge. They are full of water to hold the plant upright.

TUBES IN THE PLANT

Some cells join together to make tubes. Some of the tubes carry water up from the root to the leaves on the shoot. They have strong walls which also help to hold up the shoot. Another set of tubes carry food made in the leaves to other parts of the plant.

The tubes which carry water in woody stems are arranged in a ring. Each year the stem grows a new ring of tubes.

▌INVESTIGATE!

The stringy threads in a celery stalk are groups of tubes that carry water. Put some ink in a glass of water and stand a celery stalk in it. After half an hour, see how far the ink has gone up the tubes in the stalk.

The cells in this stem have joined together to form tubes.

How plants make food

Plants use the energy in the sunlight to turn water, carbon dioxide and minerals into food. This process of using light to make food is called photosynthesis.

Trapping energy

A green plant makes most of its food in its leaves. The cells in the leaf contain small discs called chloroplasts which are filled with a green pigment called chlorophyll. The chlorophyll absorbs energy from sunlight.

The leaf's water supply

The plant needs water, and minerals dissolved in water, to photosynthesise. The plant draws water and minerals from the soil in through its roots. The water flows upwards through the tiny tubes in the root and shoot.

Some water escapes through holes in the leaves called stomata (sig. stoma). This causes more water to be pulled up through the roots.

sunlight

chloroplasts

transparent cells forming skin

stoma

GREEN PLANTS AND AIR

The leaf takes in a gas from the air called carbon dioxide. The energy from sunlight is used to change the carbon dioxide and water into a food called carbohydrate and a gas called oxygen. The oxygen passes out of the leaf into the air.

Bubbles of oxygen have left this water plant after photosynthesis.

→ *water*
→ *food*

The food made in the leaves is transported to other parts of the plant by tiny tubes in the shoot.

▌INVESTIGATE!

Cut a hole in the side of a cardboard box and put it over a pot of seedlings. Leave it for a few days, and then see how the seedlings have grown to the light passing through the hole.

THE PARTS OF A FLOWER

A plant can make its own food, but it needs help to reproduce. Flowering plants make seeds to reproduce. Before a seed can be made, pollen must be moved from one part of a flower to another. This process is called pollination.

INSECT-POLLINATED PLANTS

Insect-pollinated plants use insects to carry the pollen from one flower to another. They attract insects to the flower with bright petals and sweet nectar.

Petals.

Sepals. They protected the flower when it was a bud.

Stigma. It receives pollen.

Style.

Stamens. The swollen tip is called an anther. It makes pollen.

Ovary. It contains smaller structures called ovules. Each ovule can produce a seed.

At the base of the flower are nectaries which make nectar.

florets

FLORETS

Some plants make many small flowers called florets which form a group called a flowerhead like this gerbera.

carpels

CARPELS

Some flowers, such as the celandine, do not have an ovary. Instead, they have a number of small structures called carpels. Each one contains an ovule which can become a seed.

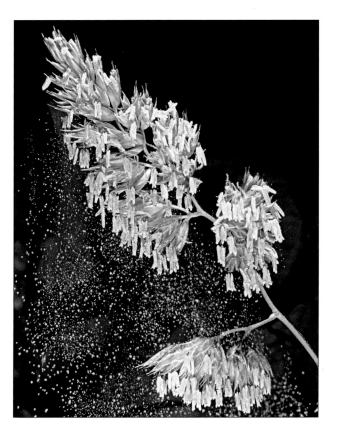

WIND-POLLINATED FLOWERS

Wind-pollinated flowers use the wind to blow pollen from one flower to another.

These flowers do not have petals or nectaries, but they do have stamens and an ovary. The stamens have long stalks and hang outside the flower so the wind can blow away the pollen. The stigma also hangs outside the flower to catch pollen floating in the wind.

Grass flowers grow together at the top of a stalk. These have hung out their anthers to release their pollen.

POLLINATION

A grain of pollen contains a nucleus of a cell. This nucleus has to reach the stigma of a flower to help the plant reproduce. Pollination is the process in which the pollen moves from an anther to a stigma.

INSECT POLLINATION

Most flowers are pollinated by insects. The insects are attracted to the flowers to feed. The pollen grains of insect-pollinated flowers have spikes covering their surfaces. When an insect such as a bee visits a flower with ripe anthers, the pollen spikes stick to the hairs on the bee's body.

A bee picks up pollen as it brushes past the anthers to feed on the nectar.

The pollen stays on the bee until it reaches a flower with a sticky stigma. As the bee goes down into the flower to feed on the nectar, the sticky stigma pulls the pollen off the bee's hairs.

The spikes on the pollen's surface make it cling to the insect's hairs as the insect flies between flowers.

INVESTIGATE!

Look at the flowers of plants around your home or school. Find the stigma and the anthers.

WIND POLLINATION

The pollen from wind-pollinated flowers is very light so that it can be carried away by very gentle winds. The flowers make lots of pollen to increase the chance of some pollen reaching another flower.

The pollen is released into the air by the anther of one flower and is caught by the stigma of another flower. The stigmas on wind-pollinated flowers have many fine strands like a feather which form a net to catch pollen blowing by.

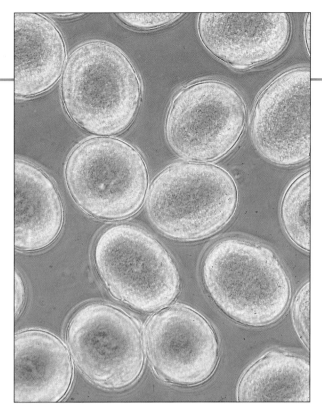

The pollen of wind-pollinated flowers have smooth surfaces because they do not need to grip onto an animal's body.

CROSS POLLINATION

It is possible for plants to pollinate themselves. Pollen can travel from an anther to a stigma on the same flower. This is called self pollination. If the anther and the stigma are on separate flowers, it is called cross pollination. Cross pollination produces plants which may survive better than plants produced by self pollination.

HOW A SEED IS MADE

After pollination, the nucleus in the pollen grain must reach a nucleus in an ovule. Once this has happened, an ovule can become a seed.

FERTILIZATION

When a pollen grain lands on a stigma, a tube grows out of its side. The pollen tube grows down through the stigma and style and into an ovule in the ovary.

The nucleus in the pollen grain moves along the tube and enters the ovule. Here, it joins with another nucleus. The joining of one nucleus with another in this way is called fertilisation. Fertilisation changes the ovule into a seed.

pollen grains on stigma

style

pollen tube

ovule

LOTS OF SEEDS

There may be many pollen grains which land on a stigma. Each one can fertilize an ovule. If there are many ovules in the ovary, fertilisation may form many seeds.

Each of these peas has formed from a separate pollen grain and ovule. The ovary has become the pod.

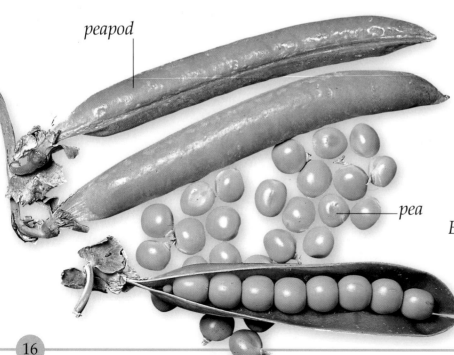

peapod

pea

CHANGES IN THE FLOWER

After fertilisation has taken place, the flower is no longer needed and its petals and stamens dry up and fall off. The ovary changes its shape and colour and becomes a fruit. Some fruits like the tomato take in water and form a fleshy wall around the seeds.

Remains of the flower.

The kiwi fruit, avocado, orange and tomato are all fruits with fleshy walls.

INVESTIGATE!

The tomato is a fruit. Cut a tomato open and see how the seeds are arranged inside it. How many seeds are there in a tomato?

FRUITS

A fruit forms from an ovary. It contains one or more seeds and it helps them to spread out, or disperse, from the parent plant. Seeds need to spread out, so that the plants that grow from them do not compete with each other for space, water and light.

FRUITS AND ANIMALS

Some fruits can be dispersed by sticking to animals. They have hooks and spines that stick to fur and feathers. Mammals and birds pick them up on their bodies as they brush against the parent plant. The fruits may be carried many kilometres before they drop off.

This burdock fruit will travel far from the parent plant on this dog's fur.

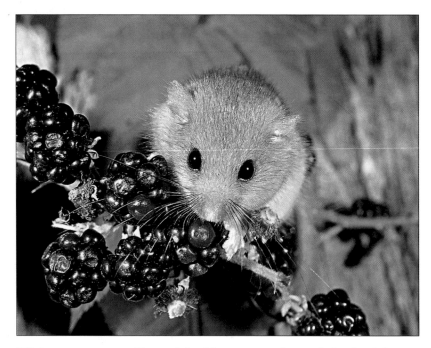

This mouse swallows blackberry seeds and fruit. The seeds will be dispersed in the mouse's droppings.

The seeds from many fruit are dispersed by passing through the body of an animal. These seeds develop in fruits which produce a soft, tasty substance around the seeds to attract animals. When the animal eats the fruit, it swallows the seeds. The seeds leave the animal in its droppings far from the parent plant.

A gust of wind can push so strongly on the dandelion fruits that they break free and scatter.

FRUIT IN THE AIR

Fruits which use the air to carry them, grow special parts to increase their air resistance. This makes the fruit and the seed fall more slowly and be carried further on the wind. Some fruits, like the maple, have wings, while fruits like the dandelion have a tuft of hairs, these act as a parachute.

These sycamore fruits spin like helicopter rotors.

▌INVESTIGATE!

Make a model of a winged fruit from a piece of paper 6 cm long and 4 cm wide. Screw up about 2 cm of one end of the paper and tear the other end to make two wings 2 cm wide. Drop your fruit and see it spin. How does changing the size of the wings change the way the model fruit spins?

SEEDS

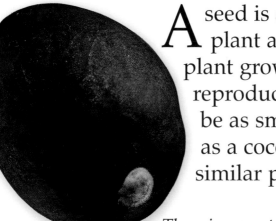

A seed is a capsule that contains a tiny plant and a store of food to help the plant grow. Flowering plants and conifers reproduce by making seeds. A seed may be as small as a speck of dust or as large as a coconut, but all seeds have the similar parts.

There is a great range in the size and shape of seeds.

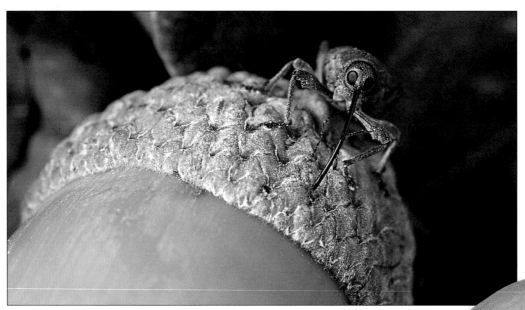

The insect is unable to get through the strong coat of this acorn.

THE SEED COAT

The tiny plant and its food store are covered by a seed coat. This forms a hard surface which prevents many kinds of insects from biting their way into the seed and feeding on its contents.

The scar on the seed coat of this broad bean shows where it was attached to the ovary.

INSIDE A SEED

In many seeds, such as the broad bean seed, there are two large food stores. Between them is one tiny plant called an embryo plant. It looks a little like a walking stick. The 'handle' is the tiny shoot and the straight part of the 'stick' is the tiny root. Each food store is connected to the embryo plant by a short stalk.

tiny plant

food store

WHY SEEDS ARE DRY

Before the seed leaves the plant, most of the water it contains is removed. This stops the seed from going mouldy. The seed coat prevents water from entering the seed and it remains unharmed in the soil until it is time for the tiny plant to grow.

INVESTIGATE!

The appearance, size and weight of a seed changes as it takes in water. Put some dry pea seeds or bean seeds in water for a day and see how they change.

SEEDS IN THE SOIL

Some seeds may stay in the soil for many years without taking in water. They are said to be dormant. The seed will stay dormant in the soil until the conditions are right for it to grow.

The shoots of these coconut seedlings have grown out after the roots have grown into the sand.

W hen the conditions are right, the tiny embryo plant inside the seed takes in water and begins to grow. We say the seed germinates.

WHY SEEDS NEED WATER

In the dormant seed, the cells of the embryo plant are resting and little water is needed for them.

When the embryo plant begins to grow, new cells are produced which need water to keep them alive so more water is taken into the seed. The water also lets the food move from the food stores to the embryo plant to help it to grow.

WHEN THE ROOT GROWS

The part of the embryo plant to grow first is the root. It bursts out of the seed coat and grows down into the soil. Water passes into the plant through the surface of the root. Hairs grow out of the root to increase the surface for taking up water so that plenty of water can be taken in for the rapidly-growing plant.

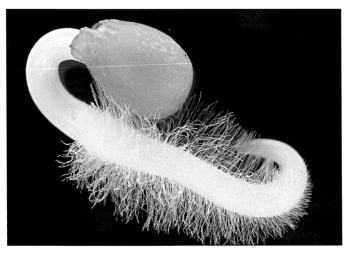

The root of this mustard seed grows out through the broken seed coat and sprouts hairs to collect water from the soil.

THE FIRST SHOOT

There are two ways in which the shoot of the embryo plant may grow. In some plants, like peas and beans, the shoot may grow out from between the food stores and push upwards through the soil and into the air.

In plants like the sunflower the shoot takes the food stores with it as it grows through the soil. When the shoot reaches the air the food stores turn green and become the first leaves.

In both kinds of plant, when the plant has grown a shoot and leaves it is called a seedling. The seedling can make its own food.

The broad bean shoot leaves the food stores behind as it grows upwards.

The leaves on this sunflower seedling are formed from the food stores which were inside the seed.

Some flowering plants also use a second method of reproducing. They make small copies of themselves. In time these new plants grow up to be identical to the parent plant.

This strawberry plant has put out a runner to produce a new plant.

GROWING OFF A STALK

The strawberry plant sends out side shoots with buds called runners. When each bud opens it forms a small plant. At first, the leaves get the water they need through the runner from the parent plant's roots. Soon the new plant grows roots to collect its own water from the soil and the runner, which is no longer needed, withers away.

POTATO TUBERS

New potato plants grow from swellings called tubers. The tubers, which we call potatoes, grow on underground side shoots. When the potato plant dies, the potatoes remain in the soil. The following year, each potato becomes a new potato plant.

This potato plant has made ten tubers.

This bud is growing into a bulb.

Two new shoots are forming inside this onion bulb.

MAKING NEW BULBS

Some plants like the tulip form a bulb. The bulb is made from parts of leaves that are swollen with food. The leaves that made the food have died away. Some of the food the leaves made is sent into buds on the stem. The buds swell up to form new bulbs. When the bulbs separate they form a group or clump of plants.

▮ INVESTIGATE!

The spider plant is a house plant grown in many homes which produces runners. Cut some small spider plants from their runners. Plant them in soil and see how they grow.

TAKING A CUTTING

A clone of some plants, such as the geranium, can be made by cutting off a leaf or a side shoot and placing it in water or damp soil. The leaf or shoot grows roots and can be grown into a new plant.

A plant's growth from seed to fully grown plant that reproduces is called its life cycle. Some plants have a life cycle which is over in a few weeks while others may live for hundreds of years.

A SHORT LIFE CYCLE

Some plants have a life cycle that is only a few weeks. These plants are called ephemerals. The seeds of ephemerals germinate soon after they are dispersed so that the life cycle of one plant can follow another through the spring to the autumn.

The Shepherd's Purse, above, is an ephemeral plant.

ONE YEAR LIFE CYCLE

Many plants complete their life cycle in one year. They are called annual plants. Their seeds are usually formed and dispersed in the autumn by the parent plants. During the winter the seeds survive in the soil and in the following spring they germinate. The seedlings grow up during the spring and the plants become full grown by the summer and produce flowers. Fruits are formed in the late summer which contain seeds for the following year. When the seeds are dispersed the plants die.

The marigolds and petunias in this flower bed are annuals.

TWO YEAR LIFE CYCLE

Plants which have a two year life cycle are called biennials. The carrot is a biennial and at the end of its first year it stores food in its root so it can use it in the following to help it grow flowers and produce seeds.

LONG-LIVED PLANTS

Plants which live for many years are called perennials. Parts of the shoot of perennial plants may die away at the end of the growing season while other parts of the shoot and the roots live on underground.

Woody flowering plants such as trees and bushes are perennials but their shoots do not die back. Their leaves fall off and the shoot is protected from the winter weather by the bark.

These carrots are being dug up to provide food for people instead of letting them grow shoots again next year.

The iris is a perennial. After its leaves die away its underground shoot and roots live in the soil through the winter.

The bark insulates these tree trunks from the cold weather.

GROWING PLANTS

Plants provide our food. Most of our meals contain parts of plants. Even meat comes from animals that have eaten plants. As the number of people on the planet continues to get larger, more and more food is needed. This can be provided by making crop plants grow as well as possible.

Many different plants are good to eat.

ADDING MINERALS

Minerals are chemicals in the soil that plants need for healthy growth. In natural habitats, such as woodlands, the minerals the plants take from the soil passes back into the soil again when the plant dies. When crop plants are grown, they are taken away to be eaten and the amount of minerals in the soil falls. Manure from animals, or fertilisers made in the chemical industry, are spread on the soil to put the minerals back.

PESTICIDES

The growth of a plant can be slowed down by insects or fungi growing on it, or by weeds taking the minerals from the soil around it. The insects, fungi and weeds are called pests, and to get rid of pests, farmers treat crops with pesticides. Pesticides are chemicals that kill the pests but leave the crops unharmed.

Spraying pesticides keeps the crop growing well.

■ INVESTIGATE!

Germinate seeds in two plant pots and when the seedlings start growing cover one of the pots with an upturned transparent jar. Compare how the two pots of seedlings grow on a sunny window-sill.

GREENHOUSES

A greenhouse traps heat energy from the Sun inside it and this warms the air, soil and plants. The warmth makes the plants grow faster. It also keep the plants growing when it is too cold for them to survive outside.

These plants are thriving in the warm sunny greenhouse.

GLOSSARY

ALGAE – green plants without flowers that are mainly very small and live in water.

ANTHER – the part of the flower that makes pollen.

BUD – a structure on the shoot from which side shoots, leaves and flowers may grow.

CAPSULE – a container.

CELL – a tiny living structure. The bodies of plants and animals are made up from large numbers of cells.

CHLOROPHYLL – a green substance found in leaves which absorbs some of the energy in sunlight.

CHLOROPLAST – a structure in a plant cell which contains chlorophyll.

CLONE – a plant or an animal which is identical to its parent.

CONIFER – a woody plant with needle-like leaves which bears cones instead of flowers. Most conifers make their seeds in the cones.

CROP – a plant grown to provide food for people or animals.

CROSS POLLINATION – the transfer of pollen from the flower of one plant to the flower of another plant of the same kind.

FERN – a non-flowering plant which has large feather-like leaves called fronds.

FERTILISATION – the process in which the nucleus from the pollen joins with a nucleus in the ovule to make a seed.

FERTILISER – a substance which is made from chemicals that contains the minerals a plant needs for growth.

FLOWERING PLANT – a plant with root, stem and leaves which reproduces by means of flowers.

GERMINATION – the process in which a seed breaks open and the plant it contains begins to grow.

HABITAT – a place such as a woodland or a pond where plants and animals live.

LEAF – a structure on a plant which makes food.

MANURE – the dropping of animals which are spread on the soil to give it extra minerals.

MINERALS – chemicals in the soil that the plant needs for healthy growth.

MOSS – small plants with stems and leaves but without proper roots.

NECTAR – a liquid containing sugar which provides food to insects visiting flowers.

NECTARY – a structure at the bottom of a flower that produces nectar.

NUCLEUS – the structure in a cell which controls the cell's activities.

OVARY – a part of the flower that contains the ovules. After fertilisation, it forms the fruit which contains the seeds.

OVULE – a structure inside the ovary which becomes a seed once it has been fertilised.

PETAL – the part of the flower that attracts insects to it by its colour.

POLLEN – tiny grains made by the anther of a flower. Each grain contains a nucleus.

POLLINATION – the transfer of pollen from an anther to a stigma.

REPRODUCE – to make new individuals such as the young in animals or seedlings in plants.

ROOT – the part of the plant which grows underground. It holds the plant in the ground and collects water and minerals for it to make food.

SEED – a structure which contains a tiny plant and its food store.

SELF POLLINATION – the transfer of pollen from the anther of a flower to its stigma or to the stigma of another flower on the same plant.

SHOOT – the part of the flowering plant above the ground which includes the stem, branches, leaves and flowers.

SPORE – a tiny structure which contains part of a non-flowering plant such as a moss or a fern and travels in the air, settles on the ground and grows into a new plant.

STAMEN – the part of the flower which is made up from the anther and the stalk that supports it.

STEM – the part of the shoot which supports branches, leaves and flowers.

STIGMA – the part of the flower that receives the pollen grains.

STYLE – the stalk that connects the stigma to the ovary.

INDEX